D060232C

Baby Elephants at the Zoo

Eustacia Moldovo

Enslow Publishing
101 W. 23rd Street
Suite 240
New York, NY 10011
USA
enslow.com

Published in 2016 by Enslow Publishing, LLC.
101 W. 23rd Street, Suite 240, New York, NY 10011

Copyright © 2016 by Enslow Publishing, LLC.
All rights reserved.

No part of this book may be reproduced by any means without the written permission of the publisher.

Library of Congress Cataloging-in-Publication Data
Moldovo, Eustacia.
 Baby elephants at the zoo / Eustacia Moldovo.
   pages cm. — (All about baby zoo animals)
 Audience: Age 4-6.
 Audience: K to Grade 3.
 Includes bibliographical references and index.
 Summary: "Describes the life of an elephant calf at a zoo, including its behaviors, diet, and physical traits"—Provided by publisher.
 ISBN 978-0-7660-7091-2 (library binding)
 ISBN 978-0-7660-7089-9 (pbk.)
 ISBN 978-0-7660-7090-5 (6-pack)
 1. Elephants—Infancy—Juvenile literature. 2. Zoo animals—Juvenile literature. I. Title.
 QL737.P98M6355 2016
 599.6713'92—dc23
                              2015000145

Printed in the United States of America

To Our Readers: We have done our best to make sure all Web sites in this book were active and appropriate when we went to press. However, the author and the publisher have no control over and assume no liability for the material available on those Web sites or on any Web sites they may link to. Any comments or suggestions can be sent by e-mail to customerservice@enslow.com.

Photo Credits: Alan Jeffery/Shutterstock.com, p. 14; Allison Coyle/Shutterstock.com, p. 22; Colette3/Shutterstock.com, p. 8; Eric Robinson/iStock/Thinkstock, p. 20; Lucy Liu/Shutterstock.com, p. 10; MyImages – Micha/Shutterstock.com, pp. 4–5; Stephaniellen/Shutterstock.com, pp. 3 (left), 6; Tanya Puntti/Shutterstock.com, p. 1; TippaPatt/Shutterstock.com, pp. 3 (right), 18; Waddell Images/Shutterstock.com, pp. 3 (center), 16; worradirek/Shutterstock.com, p. 12.

Cover Credits: Allison Coyle/Shutterstock.com, p. 22 (elephant calf in enclosure); Nelson Marques/Shutterstock.com (baby blocks on spine).

Contents

Words to Know 3

Who Lives at the Zoo? 5

Read More 24

Web Sites 24

Index 24

Words to Know

calf   herd   trunk

Who lives at the zoo?

A baby elephant lives at the zoo!

A baby elephant is called a calf.

An elephant calf is gray. Its skin is thick and has hair.

An elephant calf has a trunk. The trunk helps the elephant calf breathe and grab toys and food.

An elephant calf uses its trunk to spray water on itself. It loves to take baths!

An elephant calf lives
with its family at the zoo.
A family of elephants is
called a herd.

An elephant calf eats bananas. It also eats other fruits, leaves, twigs, and grass.

An elephant calf holds
on to its mother's tail.
It walks behind her when
the herd moves.

You can see an elephant calf at the zoo!

Read More

Lindeen, Mary. *Elephants*. Minneapolis, Minn.: Bullfrog Books, 2013.

Rustad, Martha E. H. *Elephants Are Awesome!* Mankato, Minn.: Capstone Press, 2015.

Web Sites

San Diego Zoo Kids: African Elephant
kids.sandiegozoo.org/animals/mammals/african-elephant

Earth's Kids: Elephants
earthskids.com/ek-elephants.aspx

Index

bath, 15

calf, 9, 11, 13, 15, 17, 19, 21, 23

hair, 11

herd, 17, 21

mother, 21

skin, 11

tail, 21

toys, 13

trunk, 13, 15

zoo, 5, 7, 17, 23

Guided Reading Level: D
Guided Reading Leveling System is based on the guidelines recommended by Fountas and Pinnell.

Word Count: 123